WORLD'S
BEST PIZZA

Johnny Di Francesco

WORLD'S
BEST PIZZA

Johnny Di Francesco

NEW HOLLAND

CONTENTS

INTRODUCTION

When people ask how I got into the business of pizza, I think they are often surprised by my response. I may be Italian, and my heritage may be from Campagna which is considered the home of pizza, but it was neither a love of food, nor a burning desire to embrace my history that led me down this path. It was a pair of sneakers.

When I was 12 I desperately wanted a pair of Nikes, but unfortunately new sneakers for the sake of fashion just wasn't something that my family could afford. That was a pivotal moment for me, and I started working at a pizzeria after school so I could earn enough money to buy the shoes myself. I guess from that point the cliché of 'and the rest is history' rings fairly true.

That said, my start in the world of pizza most certainly wasn't a glamorous one. I started at the bottom, washing dishes, and slowly started to work my way up the ranks. And when I say slowly, I really do mean slowly! By the time I hit 15 I had been working for three years and I started to get more involved with the kitchen. I loved the energy, the passion, and watching the pizzas evolve from nothing at all to this amazing, varied cuisine that people couldn't get enough of. By 17 I was given the chance to manage my own pizza section at a restaurant in Carlton, and I was also about to enter university around the same time. I was accepted into electronics engineering and started my degree. I went to university during the day, and I continued to work in the pizza restaurant at night. One day during my first year, I was sitting in a lecture and all I could think about was getting to the pizza shop. I was thinking that the dough needed to be taken out, about what prep needed to be done for the night ahead – I was thinking about all things pizza, and nothing remotely related to electronics engineering. I still remember gathering my things that day, putting my hand up to excuse myself to go to the bathroom, and then never returning.

My mum wasn't thrilled when I told her about my decision. I went home and told her I was quitting university and was going to open a pizza shop, which was not what she was hoping for, or happy to hear. But with that, I started to look for premises. I found an empty shop in Moonee Ponds, naively took on a massive lease and my mum agreed to guarantor the loan for me. Despite my very good intentions and my business ambitions, I quickly learned that you can't set up a pizzeria with the money that I had available to me! I worked incredibly hard to overcome the financial issues I was having, and built the business to a point where it was sellable only ten months later. I was 20.

By this time, I was well aware that business was a lot of hard work, but I was also a big believer *in* hard work, and I still believe that if you add creativity to that, you can be successful. After selling Moonee Ponds, I looked for another location, and I actually found two – one in Brunswick and one in Campbellfield. The owner of the premises in Campbellfield was operating a take-away business, and he agreed to sell the shop to me with the understanding that I would commence paying for it six months later. To this day, I have no idea why he agreed to it, especially as he was fairly opposed to me making any changes to the existing fit out and operating procedures.

Despite his reservations, I made the changes and kept him on as an employee. Within months, I had increased the turnover of the business five fold, and I sold my other store in Brunswick in order to focus on the take-away business.

Buoyed by the success of the Campbellfield store, I opened five other sites over the course of the following seven to eight years, and by the age of 27 I was running six premises. In hindsight I guess this was the start of Gradi Group which operates today. Through managing multiple locations, I also finally learned that there's more to a good pizza restaurant than just good pizza. Although the quality of the end product remains at the heart of the experience, there is so much more involved to get to that point, and to ensure your restaurant can actually provide that – something which took me a long time to learn! Systems, processes, training, staff – it's a long list, but a lot goes into what many consider to be the simple dish presented at the table.

The seven-year period between my being 21 and 28 was without doubt the most difficult of my life. The hours involved with managing six locations were unthinkable, and I spent the entire time living off credit cards. I was married with a young family – my first child arrived on the scene when I was 23, and the level of commitment I needed to keep the businesses running meant I saw my kids a lot less than I would have liked. My wife Maria is a saint, what more can I say!

The frenetic pace and lack of time to spend with my family started to take its toll, and by the time I reached 30, I started to sell off sites. I kept Campbellfield, and I still own it to this day. In fact, I visit that shop daily. For me, it's where it all started – without that take-away business, I would not be where I am today, and for that reason I can't part with it. It's a massive piece of the Gradi puzzle and it's also a humbling reminder of where things began.

After selling the majority of the businesses, I was asked a lot about what I was going to do next, and my answer was that I wanted to do something special. I wanted to bring something to Australia that hadn't been seen before. That something was the pizza of Naples. Until this point, the pizza we were making was very much 'Australian', and the traditional pizza of Naples couldn't be more different from what our customers were eating. I had one of these conversations with the agent that sold my shops for me, and incredibly he's the one who found me a site to start building my dream – and that site is now 400 Gradi in Brunswick. With the location sorted, I began perfecting the art of Neapolitan pizza, determined to introduce it into the mouths and hearts of Victorians.

My enthusiasm was quickly tested, and I spent the first 18 months of operating thinking I'd made the biggest mistake of my life. I had naively assumed that my passion and love for Neapolitan pizza would be shared, but people just didn't understand what I was trying to do. They didn't understand this 'soggy' pizza that was being presented to them because it was so different to what they were used to, and so different to what they were expecting.

I remember the first restaurant review that 400 Gradi received. It wasn't good. I read it and felt almost beaten – here was someone professing to be an expert in food, but who didn't understand the basics of Neapolitan pizza, or what we were trying to achieve. I was deflated, but incredibly that bad review worked to our advantage and it put the restaurant on the map. People started to come in, I think to see if our pizza was really as bizarre and bad as the food critic had claimed it to be. It seemed that a lot of people wanted to come to see for themselves what exactly I was doing to their beloved pizza, and the other type of people who started to come were the travellers. Australians are well travelled, and people who had been to Naples and who had experienced this type of pizza were excited by the prospect of being able to order it at home. That bad review was a turning point for us, and for that reason I can never be angry about it.

As our reputation began to grow I started to formally train in the art of Neapolitan pizza so that I could really educate people, and really communicate to people what's so special about this pizza. This was an incredible and historic journey for me personally as it gave me the opportunity to discover more about my own heritage while I gained a better understanding of the food I was trying to introduce from Naples. Educating people is still a really important aspect of what I do, and it's why I started running master classes at 400 Gradi. I want to share the history behind what we do every day, I want to impart the passion that comes with a tradition that is thousands of years old, and mostly I want people to make their own really delicious pizza!

Much of my training was undertaken with the *Verace Pizza Napoletana* (VPN), which is an international association dedicated to promoting Neapolitan pizza traditions – and it's serious training! They give lectures, they take you out to flour mills and Mozzarella producers, and you spend hours upon hours making pizza under the supervision of their master pizzaiolos. At night they send you out to work in historic pizzerias throughout the city, and it's fascinating – these guys could stick their finger in dough and tell when it was ready to be cooked. In a city where the volume of flour used has to change daily depending on the level of humidity in the air, you really do see firsthand how much of an art creating a Neapolitan pizza is. The nerve-wracking ending to the

training involves a written and practical exam where VPN judges scrutinize every aspect of your cooking – it's like being on a talent show for pizza chefs!

I loved the training, and whilst I've had a few career highlights in my time, being awarded the position of Australasian Principal of the VPN is definitely one of them. This training gave me the confidence to start entering into pizza making competitions, and in 2010 I entered my first competition in Naples. It was a ridiculously hot day – 47°C – and trying to make dough in the heat was close to impossible – so impossible that the dough I was working with literally exploded. I competed already devastated as I knew that the dough wasn't right, it wasn't what I wanted to present, and it wasn't a true reflection of what I can do in the kitchen. I flew home from that competition trying to tell myself that it was a learning experience, but I was so disappointed in myself that I didn't compete again for several years.

Following that disastrous competition, I joined the Australian pizza team and rather than put my pizza making skills out to be judged solo, I went back to Italy to compete as part of the Australian team. We didn't get a result, but this time I wasn't disappointed or disheartened when we came home, and I think being part of a team gave me the confidence boost I needed to consider competing again.

Despite not winning any competitions, my training and the now busy 400 Gradi thankfully meant that people did recognize my understanding of Naples' traditional pizza. As a result, I was asked to judge the 2013 Australian Cup. Following this, I wanted to try and gain the type of awareness I'd been hoping for through competing in the international arena, and in early 2014 I travelled to the US to compete in the Las Vegas competition. The Vegas competition is one of the biggest in the world, and I came third. After my earlier competition experiences, third place may as well have been first for me. I was thrilled and it was great for my confidence. All I could think was, I can make a pizza under pressure after all!

Not long after competing in Vegas, I flew back to the motherland to compete in The World Pizza Championship in Parma. I competed in the category that means the most to me – STG (Traditional Speciality Guaranteed or *Specialità Tradizionale Garantita*). I remember cooking as though I was cooking on Lygon Street, just focusing on putting love into the dish – and I won! I was named the maker of the best pizza in the world, which still blows my mind.

Since then, the last year has been a total whirlwind of setting up Gradi at Crown, opening my Cicchetti bar next door to 400 Gradi, and now looking to establish another restaurant in Essendon. It's non-stop but it's an absolute joy and I feel privileged to have had the experiences I have had, and to be where I am.

At the end of the day, I just love making great traditional Neapolitan pizza. I put my heart and soul into the food that I make, and having made pizza since I was 12, my passion has only intensified over time. I feel truly blessed to be able to do what I love every day, and I hope that this book and my recipes bring some of that joy into your home. Pizza is a food that is very much about sharing and bringing people together. I am so happy to share my recipes so that others can come together to enjoy not just the end result, but the magical process of traditional Neapolitan pizza.

BASIC DOUGH

When it comes to making dough, the word basic is so misleading. Dough is THE most important ingredient in any pizza, and the most important ingredient you can include is love. Take your time, treat the dough with respect, and in return you will be rewarded with a pizza base that is good enough to stand on its own.

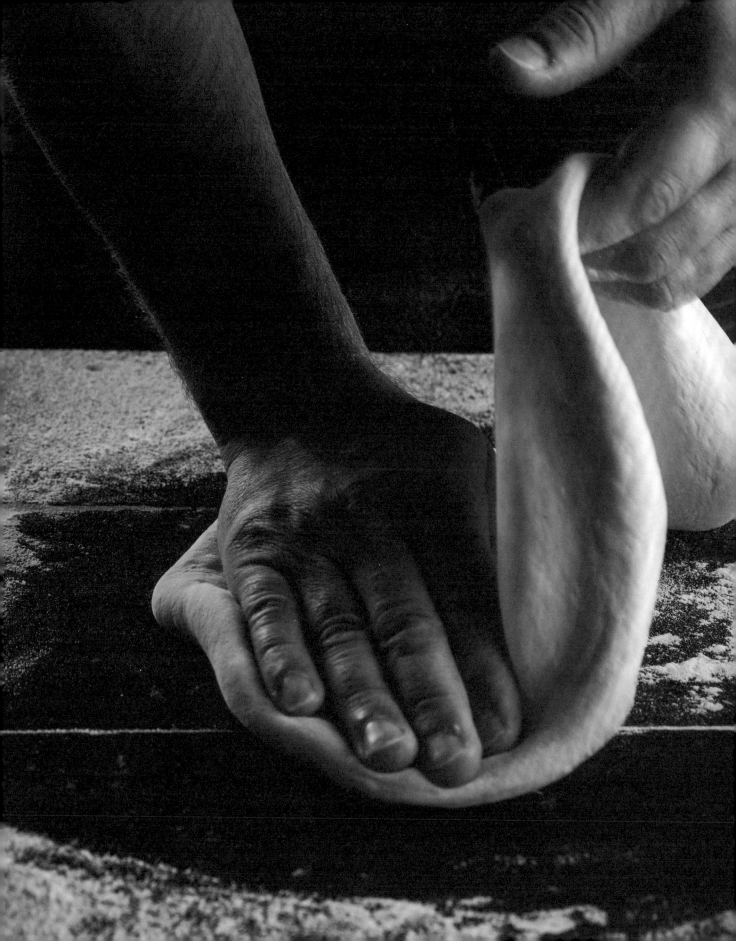

IMPASTO (dough)

Makes 10–12 bases

Ingredients

STG PIZZA NAPOLETANA DOUGH INGREDIENTS

- 1.7kg (4 lb) flour (00 5 Stagioni Pizza Napoletana flour with a W280–330)

- 1 litre (2 pints) water
- 50 g (2 oz) fine sea salt
- 1–3 g fresh yeast

Method

1. Weigh out all the ingredients.
2. Using a dough mixer mix together the water and the salt. If you don't have a machine mixer this recipe works just as well by hand, simply follow the same process as instructed below but knead by hand.
3. Start the dough mixer and then add 20% of the flour and mix.
4. Mix for 5 minutes, then add the yeast. Gradually add the remaining flour and allow to combine.
5. Once the dough has combined and seems smooth, stop the mixer, remove the dough and put aside to rest, cover with a cloth.

   Total mixing time, approximately 20 minutes. Final Dough temperature, 23–24°C (73–74°F).

6. Allow the dough to rest for approximately 2 hours, covered well at a temperature of +20°C/68°F.
7. Portion into desired dough size.
8. Round each dough piece into dough balls.
9. Place the dough balls into a sealed container, allow them to rest and rise naturally in a room no warmer than 16–18°C (60–64°F). Allow the dough to rest between 8-12 hours.

For the best cooking results:

   DOMESTIC OVEN: PRE-HEAT THE OVEN TO **220°C (425°F) AND** BAKE FOR 8–10 MINUTES
   WOOD FIRE OVEN: 90 SECONDS AT 400°C (752°F)

SENZA GLUTINE (gluten free)

Makes 10–12 bases

The following measurements are for one pack (500 g/17.5 oz) of 5 Stagioni Mix (Gluten Free), making approximately 4 pizzas. If using two packets of Stagioni Mix (1 kg/4 lb) double the ingredients, this will make approximately 9 pizzas.

Ingredients
- 435 ml (14½ fl oz) water
- 5–12.5 g yeast "instante 5 stagioni"
- 25 ml (1 fl oz) extra virgin olive oil
- 500 g (17½ oz) 5 Stagioni Mix Gluten Free (1 pack)

Method
1. Place the water and yeast in a bowl. Melt the yeast in the water using a pastry spatula.
2. Add the extra virgin olive oil to the water and yeast mixture.
3. Put the 5 Stagioni Gluten Free flour in another bowl and then add the liquid mixture.
4. Fold the mix with a plastic spatula until the mix is combined. Approximately 5–8 minutes.
5. Divide the dough pieces to your desired size and then within 1 minute mold the dough pieces into dough balls.
6. Allow the dough balls to rest for 30 minutes at a temperature of approximately 24°C (75°F).
7. When you come to use the dough balls, you must shape each dough piece again, this will release any gas held in the dough. During the resting the dough will create these gases and the dough will become rough. Once the dough has been shaped again the dough balls should be velvety and smooth.
8. By hand, gently stretch each dough ball onto an oiled tray.
9. Once stretched, precook the base at 310°C (590°F), either with a tomato base or some olive oil for approximately 3 minutes. Take the pizza base off the tray and allow to rest.
10. Add all your desired ingredients.
11. Finish off cooking for an additional 3–6 minutes.

IMPASTO INTEGRALE (wholemeal)

Makes up to 20 pizza bases

Making a perfect wholemeal dough can take up to two days. When making wholemeal pizza dough, there are two parts to the process. The first part is the biga. Biga is a type of pre-fermentation used in Italian baking, which adds complexity to the bread's taste. The second part is the dough making. Take your time as this dough is amazing when done right. Remember; great things take time. Happy dough making!

Ingredients

BIGA INGREDIENTS
- 1 kg (4 lb) 00 5 Stagioni Flour ORO
- 450 ml (15 fl oz) water
- 6 g fresh yeast

Mixing Time: 9 minutes.
Biga Temperature: 20°C (60°F)
Resting Time: 22 hours at +22°C (71°F),
place in a plastic container with a lid

DOUGH INGREDIENTS
- 1.75 kg (3.8 lb) flour
- 1 litre (2 pints) water
- BIGA (left)
- 65 g (2½ oz) fine sea salt
- 4 g fresh yeast

METHOD FOR BIGA
1. Weigh out all the ingredients.
2. Combine the flour and the yeast
3. Add the water to the dry ingredients and mix for 9 minutes.

You will find that the mix is quite hard, this is fine. Mix for no longer than 9 minutes and rest for 22 hours at +22°C (71°F), place in a plastic container with a lid.

METHOD FOR DOUGH
1. Weigh out all the ingredients.
2. Start with the Biga you made previously. Place the yeast and flour in the dough mixer.
3. Start the dough mixer and add 90% of the water, water temperature should be calculated using the formula below (this formula works well for spiral mixers).

Formula:
Starting number: 56
Calculate: Flour; Ambient temperature, Heat transfer from mixer = Water

For example:
Flour: 20°C
Ambient Temp: 20°C
Heat transfer: 8°C
56 – (Flour + Ambient + Heat transfer) = Water
56 – 20 – 20 – 8 = 8
Water = 8°C

4.   Mix for 3 minutes, then add the remaining 10% of the water and allow to combine for
     2 minutes.
5.   Add all the salt.
6.   Once the dough has combined and seems smooth, stop the mixer, remove the dough and put
     aside to rest, cover with a cloth.

Mixing Time: 16–18 minutes.
Final Dough Temperature: 23–24°C (73–75°F)
Resting Time: approximately 1 hour, covered well at +20°C (68°F)

7.   Portion into desired dough size.
8.   Round each dough piece into dough balls.
9.   Place the dough balls into a sealed container, allow them to rest in an ambient temperature
     and allow them to rise 50% in volume.
10. Once the dough balls have risen 50% in volume, place the container in the fridge (temperature
     between 2–3°C/35–37°F). This will allow the dough balls to continue to rise in a consistant
     shape.

*After 30 hours in the refrigerator you will have perfectly risen dough balls, in this case you will be able to utilize
the dough balls directly from the fridge without allowing them to reach room temperature.*

STARTERS

What better way to start a meal than with a variation of pizza. Turn your traditional starter on its head and serve your guests an entrée they'll never forget. From bite sized taste sensations to classic starters, you'll never consider pizza just a main course again!

BRUSCHETTA PIZZA

Makes 3 Bruschetta

Ingredients

- 60 g (2 oz) x 3 dough (see page 15)
- 2 large garlic cloves, minced
- 400 g (14 oz) diced tomatoes
- 1½ tablespoons fresh basil, chopped
- 30 ml (1 fl oz) olive oil
- Salt and pepper
- 125 ml (4 fl oz) balsamic glaze

Method

1. Following the method and baking instructions for the dough on page 15.
2. While the dough is baking, mince 1 clove of garlic and add it to a medium bowl along with the diced tomatoes, chopped basil, 1 tablespoon of olive oil and salt and pepper, to taste. Set the mixture aside.
3. Remove the pizza dough from the oven.
4. Slice the tip off of the remaining garlic clove and rub over the hot pizza dough.
5. Spoon the tomato mixture over the base, then drizzle with balsamic glaze. Serve immediately.

FOCCACIA AL ROSMARINO

Makes 1 large Foccacia

Ingredients
- 100 ml (3½ fl oz) good quality olive oil
- 3 cloves of garlic, crushed (add more if desired)
- Pinch of chilli flakes
- Rosemary
- 350 g (12½ oz) pizza dough (see page 15)
- Sea salt

Method
1. If using a domestic oven pre-heat to 220°C (425°F).
2. Heat olive oil, garlic, chilli, and rosemary in a pan until warm, using a low heat. Once warm, turn off the heat and leave to infuse for 10 minutes.
3. Roll out the fully risen dough ball.
4. Using a spoon generously cover the base of the pizza with the oil mixture.
5. Sprinkle the base with sea salt.

   DOMESTIC OVEN: BAKE IN THE PRE-HEATED OVEN FOR 8–10 MINUTES
   WOOD FIRE OVEN: 90 SECONDS AT 400°C (752°F)

6. Bake until the base is golden brown and crispy.

FOCACCIA ALL'AGLIO

Makes 1 large Foccacia

Ingredients
- 1 garlic clove, minced
- 30 ml (1 fl oz) extra virgin olive oil
- 350 g (12½ oz) pizza dough (see page 15)
- 1 sprig of rosemary, chopped
- Pinch of oregano
- Sea Salt

Method
1. If using a domestic oven pre-heat to 220°C (425°F).
2. To make the infused garlic oil, add the olive oil and the minced garlic to a pan and cook on a low heat for 10 minutes. Set aside to cool.
3. Roll out the pizza dough on to a baking tray or on a pre-heated pizza stone.
4. Smear the garlic oil over the pizza dough and sprinkle with the rosemary and the oregano.

   DOMESTIC OVEN: BAKE IN THE PRE-HEATED OVEN FOR 8–10 MINUTES
   WOOD FIRE OVEN: 90 SECONDS AT 400°C (752°F)

5. Bake until the base is golden brown and crispy. Once cooked sprinkle with sea salt.

FOCACCIA ALLE ERBE

Makes 1 large Foccacia

Ingredients

- 350 g (12½ oz) pizza dough (see page 15)
- 2–3 ml extra virgin olive oil
- 1 sprig of rosemary, chopped
- Pinch of oregano
- Sea salt

Method

1. If using a domestic oven pre-heat to 220°C (425°F).
2. Roll out the pizza dough on to a baking tray or on a pre-heated pizza stone.
3. Drizzle the olive oil over the pizza dough and sprinkle over the rosemary and oregano.

    DOMESTIC OVEN: BAKE IN THE PRE-HEATED OVEN FOR 8–10 MINUTES
    WOOD FIRE OVEN: 90 SECONDS AT 400°C (752°F)

4. Bake until the base is golden brown and crispy. Once cooked season with sea salt.

FOCACCIA CON OLIVE E POMODORINI

Makes 1 large Foccacia

Ingredients

- 350 g (12 oz) pizza dough (see page 15)
- Drizzle of extra virgin olive oil
- A handful of olives (black and green), pitted
- 10 cherry tomatoes
- 1–2 sprigs of rosemary, chopped
- Sea salt

Method

1. If using a domestic oven pre-heat to 250–280°C (500–536°F).
2. Roll out the pizza dough on to a baking tray or bench for stone cooking.
3. Smear the extra virgin olive oil over the pizza dough.
4. Evenly press the olives and cherry tomato into the pizza dough and sprinkle with rosemary.

    DOMESTIC OVEN: BAKE IN THE PRE-HEATED OVEN FOR 10 MINUTES
    WOOD FIRE OVEN: 90 SECONDS AT 400°C (752°F)

5. Once cooked sprinkle with sea salt.

PIZZA MONTANARA

I've heard people say, 'What's better than pizza? Deep fried pizza!' – and that is essentially what Pizza Montanara is, although it's not deep-fried in the traditional sense. Flash frying the dough before applying toppings gives it a richer taste and a great crunch!

POMODORO E MOZZARELLA DI BUFALA

Ingredients

- Olive oil, for frying
- ½ onion diced
- 500 g (17½ oz) San Marzano tomatoes, peeled
- Bunch of basil, chopped

- 60 g (2½ oz) x 3 dough (see page 15)
- 100 ml (3½ fl oz) extra virgin olive oil
- 120 g (4 oz) Mozzarella di Bufala
- 100g (3½ oz) Parmigiano, grated
- Salt and pepper

Method

1. In a pot, add the oil and diced onion. Simmer until transparent. Add the peeled San Marzano tomatoes to the pot and simmer for 20 minutes. Once the tomatoes have cooked, add salt and pepper to taste and the chopped basil. Stir and put aside to cool.
2. Cut the pizza dough into small circles. Pre-heat the olive oil in a deep fryer to 300°C (572°F). Carefully place the small pieces of dough in the fryer and fry until golden brown. Remember to turn the dough over as they will rise and only one side will cook.
3. Take the cooked dough out of the fryer and place onto paper towel.
4. Add the cooked tomato onto the Montanara pizza and then top with Mozzarella di Bufala, fresh basil leaves and sprinkle with grated Parmigiano.

CREMA DI ZUCCA E RUCOLA

Ingredients
- Olive oil, for frying
- 1 fresh chilli, chopped
- 1 garlic clove, chopped
- 200 g (7 oz) pumpkin, peeled and cut into cubes
- 60 g (2½ oz) x 3 dough (see page 15)
- 100 ml (3½ fl oz) extra virgin olive oil
- 50 g (2 oz) rocket (arugula)
- 50 g (2 oz) Parmigiano, grated
- Salt and pepper

Method
1. Heat the oil in a pan.
2. Add the fresh chilli, garlic and pumpkin. Gently fry off until soft. Slowly add water to keep simmering until the pumpkin is cooked. Test the pumpkin with a fork or a pointy knife to check if the pumpkin is cooked and soft.
3. Using a blender, puree the pumpkin and add salt and pepper to taste.
4. Cut the pizza dough into small circles. Pre-heat the olive oil in a deep fryer to 300°C (572°F). Carefully place the small pieces of dough in the fryer and fry until golden brown. Remember to turn the dough over as they will rise and only one side will cook.
5. Take the cooked dough out of the fryer and place onto paper towel.
6. Spread the pureed pumpkin onto the Montanara pizza.
7. Dress the rocket in a bowl with extra virgin olive oil and salt to taste, place on top of the pizza and sprinkle over the grated Parmigiano.

CREMA DI ZUCCHINE E PARMIGIANO

Ingredients

- Olive oil
- 1 fresh chilli, chopped
- 3 zucchini (courgettes), sliced
- 60 g (2½ oz) x 3 dough (see page 15)

- 100 ml (3½ fl oz) extra virgin olive oil
- 50 g (2 oz) Parmigiano, shaved
- Salt and pepper

Method

1. Heat the olive oil in a pan, add the fresh chilli and sliced zucchini. Gently fry off until nice and soft. Slowly add water to keep simmering until cooked through. Test the zucchini with a fork or a pointy knife to check it is cooked and soft.
2. In a blender, puree the zucchini with all the liquid from the pan and add salt and pepper to taste.
3. Cut pizza dough into small circles. Pre-heat the olive oil in a deep fryer to 300°C (572°F). Carefully place the small pieces of dough in the fryer and fry until golden brown. Remember to turn the dough over as they will rise and only one side will cook.
4. Take the cooked dough out of the fryer and place onto paper towel.
5. Spread the puréed zucchini onto the Montanara pizza and top with the Parmigiano.

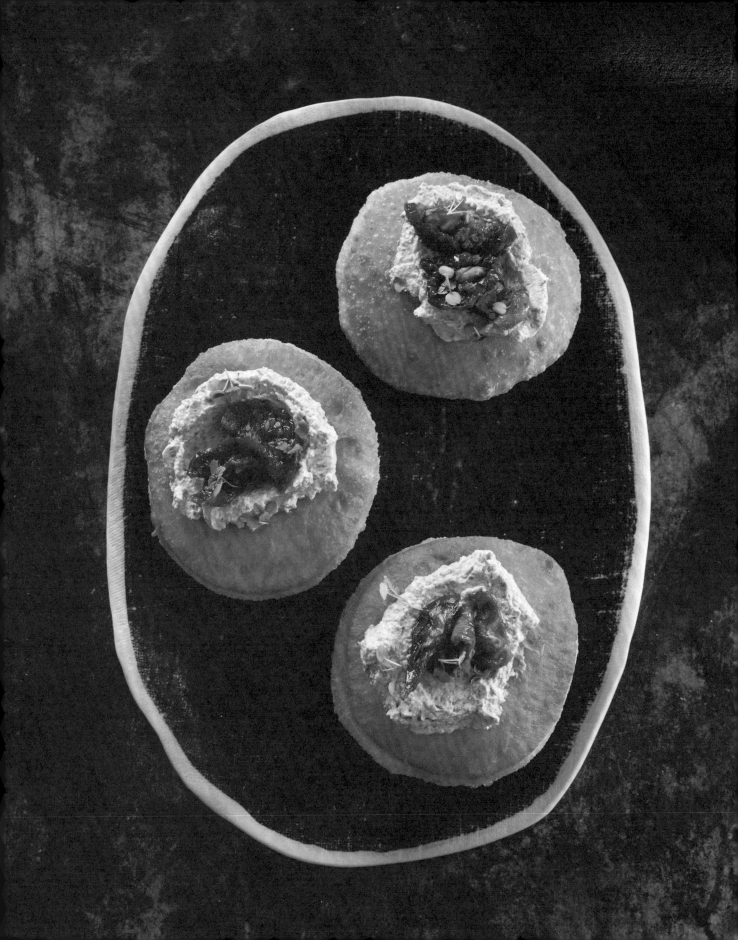

RICOTTA, PATE DI OLIVE E POMODORI SECCHI

Ingredients
- 300 g (10½ oz) Ricotta
- 100 g (3½ oz) black olives pitted
- 10 semi-dried tomatoes, chopped finely
- 100 ml (3½ fl oz) extra virgin olive oil
- 60 g (2½ oz) x 3 dough (see page 15)
- Salt and pepper

Method
1. Place the Ricotta in a bowl, season to taste and whisk until it reaches a creamy consistency. Place the Ricotta mix aside.
2. In a blender add the black olives and blend the olives while adding some extra virgin olive oil.
3. Cut the pizza dough into small circles. Pre-heat the olive oil in a deep fryer to 300°C (572°F). Carefully place the small pieces of dough in the fryer and fry until golden brown. Remember to turn the dough over as they will rise and only one side will cook.
4. Take the cooked dough out of the fryer and place onto paper towel.
5. Spread the Ricotta mix onto the Montanara pizza, dollop the olive paté in the centre and top with the semi-dried tomatoes.

CREMA DI CARCIOFI CON OLIVE NERE

Ingredients

- 10 artichoke hearts, in oil
- 60 g (2½ oz) x 3 dough (see page 15)
- 100 ml (3½ fl oz) extra virgin olive oil
- 100 g (3½ oz) black olives pitted and chopped
- Salt and pepper

Method

1. In the blender, puree the artichoke hearts in oil until a nice smooth creamy texture. Add salt and pepper to taste.
2. Cut pizza dough into small circles. Pre heat the olive oil in a deep fryer to 300°C (572°F). Carefully place the small pieces of dough in the fryer and fry until golden brown. Remember to turn the dough over as they will rise and only one side will cook.
3. Take the cooked dough out of the fryer and place onto paper towel.
4. Spread the puréed artichoke hearts onto the Montanara pizza and garnish with the chopped black olives.

CLASSIC PIZZA

For me, these classic pizzas are where my passion lies. Dating back thousands of years, the tradition found in these Neapolitan classics is a big part of what I love about pizza. Some of the following show a modern take on the classics, but what remains the same is the tradition behind the art of pizza.

THE WORLD'S BEST PIZZA MARGHERITA

WINNER
The World's Best Pizza

The classic and delicious Pizza Margherita. This is the recipe I used when competing at the Campionato Mondiale Della Pizza (Pizza World Championship) which was held in Parma, Italy. It was there and for this pizza that I was awarded the title of world's top Margherita Pizza!

Ingredients

- 220 g (8 oz) pizza dough (see page 15)
- 60 g (2½ oz) San Marzano tomatoes, peeled and crushed
- 50 g (2 oz) Buffalo Mozzarella, sliced
- 4 fresh basil leaves
- Drizzle of extra virgin olive oil

Method

1. Roll out the pizza dough on to a baking tray or bench for stone cooking.
2. Spread the San Marzano tomatoes over the dough.
3. Top with the Buffalo Mozzarella, place four basil leaves on top and drizzle with some extra virgin olive oil.

   DOMESTIC OVEN: BAKE FOR 10 MINUTES AT 250–280°C (500–536°F)
   WOOD FIRE OVEN: 90 SECONDS AT 400°C (752°F)

PIZZA MARINARA

Ingredients
- 220 g (8 oz) pizza dough (see page 15)
- 120 g (4½ oz) San Marzano tomatoes, peeled and crushed
- Sprinkle of oregano
- 3–4 garlic cloves, sliced
- Drizzle of extra virgin olive oil

Method
1. Roll out the pizza dough on to a baking tray or bench for stone cooking.
2. Spread the San Marzano tomatoes over the dough.
3. Top with the oregano and garlic then drizzle over some extra virgin olive oil.

DOMESTIC OVEN: BAKE FOR 10 MINUTES AT 250–280°C (500–536°F)
WOOD FIRE OVEN: 90 SECONDS AT 400°C (752°F)

PIZZA CON BRESAOLA

Ingredients

- 220 g (8 oz) pizza dough (see page 15)
- 60 g (2½ oz) San Marzano tomatoes, peeled and crushed
- 50g (2 oz) Buffalo Mozzarella, sliced
- 4 fresh basil leaves
- Drizzle of extra virgin olive oil
- 50 g (2 oz) Bresaola
- 20 g (¾ oz) rocket (arugula)

Method

1. Roll out the pizza dough on to a baking tray or bench for stone cooking.
2. Spread the San Marzano tomatoes over the dough.
3. Top with the Buffalo Mozzarella, place four basil leaves on top and drizzle with some extra virgin olive oil.

   DOMESTIC OVEN: BAKE FOR 10 MINUTES AT 250–280°C (500–536°F)
   WOOD FIRE OVEN: 90 SECONDS AT 400°C (752°F)

4. Once baked add the freshly sliced Bresaola and garnish with rocket that has been dressed with olive oil and salt.

PIZZA CON BEEF SALAME

Ingredients

- 220 g (8 oz) pizza dough (see page 15)
- 80 g (3 oz) San Marzano tomatoes, peeled
- 80 g (3 oz) Fior di Latte, cut into strips
- 60 g (2½ oz) Beef Salame
- Drizzle extra virgin olive oil
- 20 g (¾ oz) rocket (arugula)

Method

1. Roll out the pizza dough on to a baking tray or bench for stone cooking.
2. Spread the San Marzano tomatoes over the dough.
3. Top with Fior di Latte and place the freshly sliced Beef Salame on top.
4. Drizzle with some extra virgin olive oil.

   DOMESTIC OVEN: BAKE FOR 10 MINUTES AT 250–280°C (500–536°F)
   WOOD FIRE OVEN: 90 SECONDS AT 400°C (752°F)

5. Once baked garnish with rocket that has been dressed with olive oil and salt.

PIZZA CON BEEF NDUJA E FRIARIELLI

Ingredients

- 220 g (8 oz) pizza dough (see page 15)
- 100 g (3½ oz) Fior di Latte, cut into strips
- 60 g (2½ oz) Beef Nduja, sliced
- 90 g (3 oz) friarielli (broccoli), sliced
- Drizzle extra virgin olive oil

Method

1. Roll out the pizza dough on to a baking tray or bench for stone cooking.
2. Top with Fior di Latte, place the Beef Nduja and friarielli on top.
3. Drizzle some extra virgin olive oil.

DOMESTIC OVEN: BAKE FOR 10 MINUTES AT 250–280°C (500–536°F)
WOOD FIRE OVEN: 90 SECONDS AT 400°C (752°F)

PIZZA CON ACCIUGHE E OLIVE

Ingredients
- 220 g (8 oz) pizza dough (see page 15)
- 80 g (3 oz) San Marzano tomatoes, peeled and crushed
- 80 g (3 oz) Fior di Latte, cut into strips
- 35 g (1½ oz) olives pitted
- 35 g (1½ oz) anchovies
- Pinch of oregano
- Drizzle of extra virgin olive oil

Method
1. Roll out the pizza dough on to a baking tray or bench for stone cooking.
2. Spread the San Marzano tomatoes over the dough.
3. Top with Fior di Latte and evenly top with the olives and anchovies.
4. Sprinkle with oregano and drizzle with some extra virgin olive oil.

   DOMESTIC OVEN: BAKE FOR 10 MINUTES AT 250–280°C (500–536°F)
   WOOD FIRE OVEN: 90 SECONDS AT 400°C (752°F)

PIZZA AI FRUTTI DI MARE

Ingredients

- 220 g (8 oz) pizza dough (see page 15)
- 80 g (3 oz) San Marzano tomatoes, peeled and crushed
- 80 g (3 oz) Fior di Latte, cut into strips
- Olive oil, for frying
- 1 garlic clove, thinly sliced
- 1 fresh chilli, chopped

- 2 large prawns (shrimp), peeled
- 2 scallops, removed from their shells
- 5 vongole, in their shells
- 5 mussels, in their shells
- Parsley, chopped
- 20 g (¾ oz) rocket (arugula)

Method

1. Roll out the pizza dough on to a baking tray or bench for stone cooking.
2. Spread the San Marzano tomatoes over the dough.
3. Top with Fior di Latte and then bake the pizza.

   DOMESTIC OVEN: BAKE FOR 10 MINUTES AT 250–280°C (500–536°F)
   WOOD FIRE OVEN: 90 SECONDS AT 400°C (752°F)

While the pizza is cooking prepare the seafood.

Method for seafood

4. In a pan add the olive oil, garlic and fresh chilli (to taste). Fry until garlic becomes golden then add the prawns and scallops.
5. Cook for 30 seconds then add the vongole and the mussels, toss carefully.
6. Cook for 3 minutes and then add the chopped parsley.
7. Set aside while the pizza finishes baking.
8. Once baked garnish with rocket that has been dressed with olive oil, and top with the cooked seafood mix.

PREPARING THE SEAFOOD FOR THE PIZZA CON FRUTTI DI MARE

How to Clean Mussels and Vongole

Farm-raised mussels are thankfully quite clean to begin with and don't require the rigorous individual scrubbing-under-water that wild mussels do, but you'll still have to give them a quick once over.

Step 1: Rinse and scrub as necessary

Place your mussels in a colander or bowl in the sink and run them under cold water. Rinse to get rid of any debris or seaweed on their shells. If you feel any muddy spots, rub them off under the water.

Step 2: Debeard

Mussels attach themselves to surfaces using thin, sticky membranes referred to as "beards." Most farm-raised mussels will come debearded, but you might find a couple of stubborn beards left over. When you find one, grasp it between your thumb and forefinger and pull it downwards towards the hinged-end of the mussel shell. Pull firmly until it comes out and discard.

Step 3: Check for dead ones

Mussels, clams, and other bivalves tend to gape open when they're dead, but not all gaping mussels are dead yet. Some of them are just relaxing. If you happen to spot any gaping mussels in your bowl, you can check for signs of life by squeezing them a few times or knocking them with another mussel. The mussel should slowly close itself back up. If it doesn't, you've got a dead one on your hands. Toss it in the trash and move on with your life. And that's it! Your mussels are ready to cook.

How to clean prawns (shrimp):

. *Gently hold the base of the head, twist and remove.*
. *Wedge your three middle fingers under the shell along the base and pull away the shell and legs in one piece.*
. *Squeeze the tail and the prawn will pop out – or leave on the tail for presentation.*
. *Remove the vein by gently pulling it out from the head end or make a small slit along the back.*

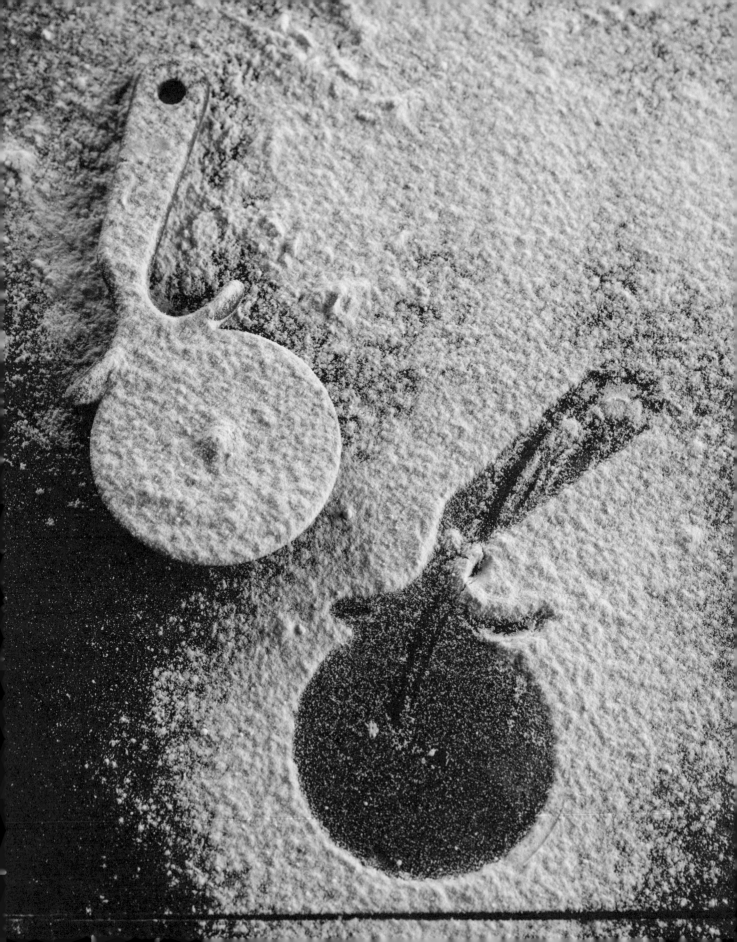

PIZZA CAPRICCIOSA

Ingredients

- 220 g (8 oz) pizza dough (see page 15)
- 80 g (3 oz) San Marzano tomatoes, peeled and crushed
- 80 g (3 oz) Fior di Latte, cut into strips
- 50 g (2 oz) Turkey ham, sliced
- 30 g (1 oz) fresh mushrooms, sliced
- 20 g (¾ oz) Ligurian olives, pitted
- 40 g (1½ oz) artichokes, chopped
- Drizzle extra virgin olive oil

Method

1. Roll out the pizza dough on to a baking tray or bench for stone cooking.
2. Spread the San Marzano tomatoes over the dough.
3. Top with Fior di Latte and place freshly sliced Turkey ham, mushrooms, olives and artichokes.
4. Drizzle with some extra virgin olive oil.

DOMESTIC OVEN: BAKE FOR 10 MINUTES AT 250–280°C (500–536°F)
WOOD FIRE OVEN: 90 SECONDS AT 400°C (752°F)

PIZZA CON TACCHINO

Ingredients

- 220 g (8 oz) pizza dough (see page 15)
- 80 g (3 oz) San Marzano tomatoes, peeled and crushed
- 80 g (3 oz) Fior di Latte, cut into strips
- 100 g (3½ oz) Turkey ham sliced
- Drizzle extra virgin olive oil

Method

1. Roll out the pizza dough on to a baking tray or bench for stone cooking.
2. Spread the San Marzano tomatoes over the dough.
3. Top with Fior di Latte and place freshly sliced turkey ham on top.
4. Drizzle some extra virgin olive oil.

DOMESTIC OVEN: BAKE FOR 10 MINUTES AT 250-280°C (500–536°F)
WOOD FIRE OVEN: 90 SECONDS AT 400°C (752°F)

PIZZA CON BRESAOLA E POMODORI SECCHI

Ingredients

- 220 g (8 oz) pizza dough (see page 15)
- 100 g (3½ oz) Fior di Latte, cut into strips
- 80 g (3 oz) Bresaola, sliced
- 60 g (2 oz) semi-dried tomatoes, sliced
- Balsamic reduction
- Drizzle extra virgin olive oil

Method

1. Roll out the pizza dough on to a baking tray or bench for stone cooking.
2. Top with Fior di Latte, drizzle with extra virgin olive oil, and bake.

   DOMESTIC OVEN: BAKE FOR 10 MINUTES AT 250–280°C (500–536°F)
   WOOD FIRE OVEN: 90 SECONDS AT 400°C (752°F)

3. Once cooked, top the pizza with the freshly sliced Bresaola, semi-dried tomatoes and drizzle with the balsamic reduction.

PIZZA AI QUATTRO FORMAGGI

Ingredients

- 220 g (8 oz) pizza dough (see page 15)
- 80 g (3 oz) Fior di Latte, cut into strips
- 60 g (2½ oz) Emmental, sliced
- 30 g (1 oz) Gorgonzola, sliced
- 10 g (½ oz) Parmigiano, grated
- Drizzle extra virgin olive oil
- 3 fresh basil leaves

Method

1. Roll out the pizza dough on to a baking tray or bench for stone cooking.
2. Top with Fior di Latte, Emmental, Gorgonzola and grated Parmigiano.

   DOMESTIC OVEN: BAKE FOR 10 MINUTES AT 250–280°C (500–536°F)
   WOOD FIRE OVEN: 90 SECONDS AT 400°C (752°F)

3. Once cooked drizzle with olive oil and garnish with the fresh basil leaves.

PIZZA PARMIGIANA

Ingredients

- 220 g (8 oz) pizza dough (see page 15)
- 90 g (3 oz) Fior di Latte, cut into strips
- 160 g (5½ oz) Parmigiana, sliced
- Drizzle extra virgin olive oil

FOR THE PARMIGIANA

- 3 eggplants (aubergine), thinly sliced
- 1 x 500 g (17 oz) tin San Marzano tomatoes, peeled
- 180 g (6 oz) Parmigiano, grated

Method

1. To make the Parmigiana, thinly slice 3 eggplants and shallow fry. Place on paper towel to absorb any excess oil.
2. In a baking tray spread the San Marzano tomatoes, layer the eggplant evenly across the tomato base. Then spread more tomato base on top of the eggplant and sprinkle the grated Parmigiano over the tomato base. Repeat this until you create three layers of eggplant.
3. Once completed bake in the oven for 20 minutes at 250°C (500 °F)
4. Roll out the pizza dough on to a baking tray or bench for stone cooking.
5. Top with Fior di Latte and Parmigiana.

   DOMESTIC OVEN: BAKE FOR 10 MINUTES AT 250–280°C (500–536°F)
   WOOD FIRE OVEN: 90 SECONDS AT 400°C (752°F)

6. Once baked drizzle with olive oil.

PIZZA ORTOLANA

Ingredients

- 30 g (1 oz) eggplant (aubergine), grilled
- 3 fresh basil leaves, chopped
- 30 g (1 oz) capsicum (bell pepper), roasted
- 1 garlic clove, minced
- 1 tablespoon olive oil
- Fresh parsley, chopped
- 60 g (2½ oz) zucchini (courgette), grilled
- Drizzle extra virgin olive oil
- Fresh mint, chopped
- 220 g (8 oz) pizza dough (see page 15)
- 90 g (3 oz) San Marzano tomatoes, peeled and crushed
- 80 g (3 oz) Fior di Latte, cut into strips
- Salt and pepper

Method

1. Thinly slice the eggplant, place onto a grill and grill each side evenly. Once grilled drizzle with olive oil, chopped basil and salt and pepper to taste.
2. Place the capsicum in a baking tray and place in a hot oven approximately 240°C (464°F) and roast until the skin appears burnt. Remove from the oven and place the roasted capsicum in a plastic bag. Tie up the bag and set aside to cool down. This will help when it comes to peeling the capsicum. Once cooled remove and discard the outer skin and chop finely. In a bowl, strain the chopped capsicum to release the juices, then add the garlic, olive oil, parsley, salt and pepper to taste.
3. Thinly slice the zucchini, place onto a grill and grill each side evenly. Once grilled drizzle with olive oil, chopped mint and salt and pepper to taste.
4. Roll out the pizza dough on to a baking tray or bench for stone cooking.
5. Top with the San Marzano tomatoes, Fior di Latte, grilled zucchini, grilled eggplant, and roasted capsicum.

DOMESTIC OVEN: BAKE FOR 10 MINUTES AT 250–280°C (500–536°F)
WOOD FIRE OVEN: 90 SECONDS AT 400°C (752°F)

I ♡ PiZZA

PIZZA CON FUNGHI E FORMAGGIO DI CAPRA

Ingredients

- 220 g (8 oz) pizza dough (see page 15)
- 110 g (4 oz) Fior di Latte, cut into strips
- 80 g (3 oz) mushrooms, sliced
- Drizzle extra virgin olive oil
- 20 g (¾ oz) rocket (arugula)
- 80 g (3 oz) Goats Cheese, crumbled

Method

1. Roll out the pizza dough on to a baking tray or bench for stone cooking.
2. Top with Fior di Latte and evenly place the freshly sliced mushrooms.
3. Drizzle wit some extra virgin olive oil.

   DOMESTIC OVEN: BAKE FOR 10 MINUTES AT 250–280°C (500–536°F)
   WOOD FIRE OVEN: 90 SECONDS AT 400°C (752°F)

4. Once baked top with the rocket that has been dressed with olive oil and sprinkle over the Goats Cheese.

PIZZA CON TONNO

Ingredients

- 220 g (8 oz) pizza dough (see page 15)
- 110 g (3½ oz) Fior di Latte, cut into strips
- 100 g (3½ oz) fresh tuna, sliced
- 80 g (3 oz) red onion, finely chopped

- Juice of 1 lemon
- Fresh parsley, chopped
- Drizzle of extra virgin olive oil

Method

1. Roll out the pizza dough on to a baking tray or bench for stone cooking.
2. Top with the Fior di Latte, place the freshly sliced tuna on the base and sprinkle the red onion on top.
3. Squeeze over some lemon juice.

    DOMESTIC OVEN: BAKE FOR 10 MINUTES AT 250–280°C (500–536°F)
    WOOD FIRE OVEN: 90 SECONDS AT 400°C (752°F)

4. Once cooked garnish the pizza with fresh parsley and drizzle with extra virgin olive oil.

PIZZA CON FICHI, MASCARPONE E BRESAOLA

Ingredients

- 220 g (8 oz) pizza dough (see page 15)
- 80 g (3 oz) Fior di Latte, cut into strips
- 3 figs, chopped
- 80 g (3 oz) Mascarpone
- 80 g (3 oz) Bresaola, sliced
- Drizzle of extra virgin olive oil

Method

1. Roll out the pizza dough on to a baking tray or bench for stone cooking.
2. Top with Fior di Latte, figs and Mascarpone.

   DOMESTIC OVEN: BAKE FOR 10 MINUTES AT 250–280°C (500–536°F)
   WOOD FIRE OVEN: 90 SECONDS AT 400°C (752°F)

3. Once cooked place freshly sliced Bresaola on top and drizzle with some extra virgin olive oil.

PIZZA CON ZUCCA

Ingredients

- 220 g (8 oz) pizza dough (see page 15)
- 10 g (½ oz) pine nuts
- Drizzle extra virgin olive oil
- 100 g (3½ oz) Fior di Latte, cut into strips
- 90 g (3 oz) pumpkin, peeled and sliced
- 20 g (¾ oz) rocket (arugula)
- 80 g (3 oz) Goats Cheese, crumbled
- Salt and pepper

Method

1. Stretch the pizza dough into a round disk.
2. Top the pizza with the pine nuts, drizzle with some extra virgin olive oil (this will ensure the pine nuts will not burn) and then top with the Fior di latte and pumpkin.

    DOMESTIC OVEN: BAKE FOR 10 MINUTES AT 280°C (536°F)
    WOOD FIRE OVEN: 90 SECONDS AT 400°C (752°F)

3. Once baked season with salt and pepper to taste and top with the rocket that has been dressed with olive oil. Finally sprinkle with Goats Cheese.

PIZZA CON TACCHINO, RUCOLA E BALSAMICO

Ingredients

- 220 g (8 oz) pizza dough (see page 15)
- 100 g (3½ oz) Fior di Latte, cut into strips
- Drizzle of extra virgin olive oil
- 90 g (3 oz) turkey ham

- 40 g (1½ oz) Raspadura, shaved
- 20 g (¾ oz) rocket (arugula)
- Drizzle of balsamic reduction

Methd

1. Stretch the pizza dough into a round disk.
2. Top pizza with Fior di latte and drizzle with some extra virgin olive oil.

   DOMESTIC OVEN: BAKE FOR 10 MINUTES AT 280°C (536°F)
   WOOD FIRE OVEN: 90 SECONDS AT 400°C (752°F)

3. Once baked top with the turkey ham, Raspadura and rocket dressed with olive oil. Finally, drizzle over the balsamic reduction.

PIZZA SOFIA LOREN

Ingredient

- 60 g (2½ oz) eggplant (aubergine), cut into strips
- 2 roman tomatoes
- 1 tablespoon icing sugar
- 220 g (8 oz) pizza dough (see page 15)
- 100 g (3½ oz) Stracciatella cheese
- Drizzle of extra virgin olive oil
- Fresh oregano, chopped
- Salt

Method

1. Cut the eggplant into strips. Place in a baking tray, drizzle with oil and season. Bake at 130°C (266°F) for 15 minutes.
2. Cut each tomato into 6 pieces. Place in a baking tray and sprinkle with icing sugar. Bake for 30 minutes at 80°C (176°F) until soft.
3. Stretch the pizza dough into a round disk. Top pizza with half the Stracciatella and place the cooked eggplant and tomatoes, drizzle with some extra virgin olive oil and bake.

   DOMESTIC OVEN: BAKE FOR 10 MINUTES AT 280°C (536°F)
   WOOD FIRE OVEN: 90 SECONDS AT 400°C (752°F)

4. Once cooked sprinkle with fresh oregano and top with the remaining Stracciatella.

PIZZA CON GAMBERI

Ingredients

- 8 tiger prawns (shrimp), peeled
- 10–20 ml olive oil
- 1 garlic clove, sliced
- 1 fresh chilli, chopped
- Fresh parsley, chopped
- 220 g (8 oz) pizza dough (see page 15)
- 80 g (3 oz) San Marzano tomatoes, peeled and crushed
- Fresh oregano, chopped
- Drizzle of extra virgin olive oil
- 6 semi-dried tomatoes, sliced

Method

1. Firstly, prepare the tiger prawns (refer to page 59 for cleaning instructions). Heat a pan with olive oil, fresh garlic and fresh chilli, add the tiger prawns and cook for approximately 3 minutes. Add the fresh parsley.
2. Stretch the pizza dough into a round disk.
3. Top pizza with San Marzano tomatoes and oregano then drizzle with extra virgin olive oil.

   DOMESTIC OVEN: BAKE FOR 10 MINUTES AT 280°C (536°F)
   WOOD FIRE OVEN: 90 SECONDS AT 400°C (752°F)

4. Once cooked top with the cooked tiger prawns and chopped semi-dried tomatoes. Serve immediately.

PIZZA CON VONGOLE

Ingredients

- 10–20 ml olive oil
- 1 garlic clove, sliced
- 1 fresh chilli, chopped
- Fresh parsley, chopped
- 12 vongole, in shells
- 220 g (8 oz) pizza dough (see page 15)
- 80 g (3 oz) San Marzano tomatoes, peeled and crushed
- Drizzle of extra virgin olive oil

Method

1. Heat the olive oil in a pan, add the garlic and fresh chilli, then add the vongole and cook for approximately 3 minutes. Add fresh parsley.
2. Stretch the pizza dough into a round disk.
3. Top the pizza with San Marzano tomatoes and a drizzle of extra virgin olive oil.

   DOMESTIC OVEN: BAKE FOR 10 MINUTES AT 250–280°C (482–536°F)
   WOOD FIRE OVEN: 90 SECONDS AT 400°C (752°F)

4. Once cooked top with cooked vongole.

PIZZA CON COZZE

Ingredients

- 10–20 ml olive oil
- 1 garlic clove, sliced
- 1 fresh chilli, sliced
- 1 roman tomato, diced
- 10 mussels, in their shells
- Fresh parsley, finely chopped
- 220 g (8 oz) pizza dough (see page 15)
- 80 g (3 oz) San Marzano tomatoes, peeled and crushed
- Drizzle of extra virgin olive oil

Method

1. Heat a pan with the olive oil, fresh garlic and fresh chilli. Add the freshly diced tomatoes and cook for approximately 3 minutes. Add the cleaned mussels (refer to page 59 for cleaning instructions) and cook for a further 3 minutes. Add the fresh parsley.
2. Stretch the pizza dough into a round disk.
3. Top pizza with San Marzano tomatoes, extra virgin olive oil and bake.

   DOMESTIC OVEN: BAKE FOR 10 MINUTES AT 250–280°C (482–536°F)
   WOOD FIRE OVEN: 90 SECONDS AT 400°C (752°F)

4. Once cooked top with the cooked mussels.

PIZZA CON FIORI DI ZUCCA

Ingredients

- 220 g (8 oz) pizza dough (see page 15)
- 80 g (3 oz) Fior di Latte, cut into strips
- 6 zucchini flowers

- 6 anchovy fillets
- Drizzle of extra virgin olive oil
- Salt and pepper

Method

1. Roll out the pizza dough on to a baking tray or bench for stone cooking.
2. Top with the Fior di Latte, and evenly place the zucchini flowers and the anchovy fillets on top.
3. Drizzle over some extra virgin olive oil and season with salt and pepper.

DOMESTIC OVEN: BAKE FOR 10 MINUTES AT 280°C (536°F)
WOOD FIRE OVEN: 90 SECONDS AT 400°C (752°F)

PIZZA CON STRACCIATELLA E ACCIUGHE

Ingredients

- 220 g (8 oz) pizza dough (see page 15)
- 100 g (3½ oz) Stracciatella cheese
- 6 anchovy fillets

- 4 fresh basil leaves
- Drizzle of extra virgin olive oil

Method

1. Roll out the pizza dough on to a baking tray or bench for stone cooking.
2. Spread the Stracciatella over the base.
3. Top with the anchovy fillets, place four basil leaves on top and drizzle with some extra virgin olive oil.

DOMESTIC OVEN: BAKE FOR 10 MINUTES AT 280°C (536°F)
WOOD FIRE OVEN: 90 SECONDS AT 400°C (752°F)

PIZZA CON ASPARAGI E SCAMORZA

Ingredients

- 150 g (5 oz) asparagus
- 1 tablespoon butter
- 3 fresh mint leaves, chopped
- Juice of 1 lemon juice
- Drizzle of extra virgin olive oil

- 220 g (8 oz) pizza dough (see page 15)
- 80 g (3 oz) Scamorza, sliced
- Parmigiano, shaved
- Parsley, chopped
- Salt and pepper

Method

1. Using a mandolin or vegetable peeler, peel each of the asparagus. Heat the butter in a pan and cook the asparagus for 3–4 minutes, season with salt and pepper. Once cooked put aside to cool down.
2. Once cooled slice the asparagus in half and place in a bowl with the chopped mint.
3. Add the lemon juice and extra virgin olive oil. Toss gently and season to taste.
4. Roll out the pizza dough on to a baking tray or bench for stone cooking.
5. Top with the Scamorza evenly, then top with the asparagus mix and a drizzle of extra virgin olive oil.

   DOMESTIC OVEN: BAKE FOR 10 MINUTES AT 280°C (536°F)
   WOOD FIRE OVEN: 90 SECONDS AT 400°C (752°F)

6. Once baked add freshly shaved Parmigiano and garnish with the freshly chopped parsley.

PIZZA CON TURKEY HAM E RICOTTA

Ingredients
- 220 g (8 oz) pizza dough (see page 15)
- 80 g (3 oz) Fior di Latte, cut into strips
- 60 g (2½ oz) Turkey ham, sliced
- 30 g (1 oz) Ricotta
- 20 g (½ oz) rocket (arugula)
- Drizzle of extra virgin olive oil

Method
1. Roll out the pizza dough on to a baking tray or bench for stone cooking.
2. Top with the Fior di Latte, and drizzle with extra virgin olive oil.

   DOMESTIC OVEN: BAKE FOR 10 MINUTES AT 280°C (536°F)
   WOOD FIRE OVEN: 90 SECONDS AT 400°C (752°F)

3. Once baked add the freshly sliced turkey ham and the Ricotta on top, then garnish the pizza with the rocket dressed with olive oil.

CALZONE

Originating in Naples, the calzone is as traditional an Italian pizza as they come. Loosely translating to "stocking" or "trouser", calzone is a stuffed pizza that roughly resembles a half moon. And your loved ones will be over the moon with these simple but delicious recipes.

CALZONE CON SCAROLA, ACCIUGHE E OLIVE

Ingredients

- Bunch of silver beet
- 100 ml (3½ fl oz) olive oil
- 1 garlic clove, sliced
- 1 pepperoncino (chilli), sliced
- 220 g (8 oz) pizza dough (see page 15)

- 60 g (2½ oz) Fior Di Latte, cut into strips
- 2 anchovies, torn into pieces
- 6 olives, pitted
- Salt and pepper

Method

1. If using a domestic oven, pre-heat to 220°C (425°F).
2. Wash the silver beet in cold water to remove any field dust and soil, chop into small pieces.
3. In a large pan, heat some olive oil, adding the garlic and pepperoncino (chilli).
4. Add the washed and chopped silver beet and stir to wilt. Season with salt and pepper. Cover to help it wilt down and cook for about 10-15 minutes or until tender.
5. Roll out a piece of dough into a 3 mm (0.1 inch) thick disc, ensure the bottom of the dough is floured enough to prevent it from sticking to the surface. On half of the dough place the Fior di Latte and the silver beet mixture leaving a 5 cm (2 in) gap around the edge. Place the anchovies, torn evenly, onto the silver beet and top with the black olives.
6. To make the calzone, carefully lift the far edge of the pizza dough and pull it over the top of the ingredients towards you, folding it in half. Crimp the edges so none of the filling can spill out.
7. Place the calzone onto a baking tray, pizza stone or granite slab.

    DOMESTIC OVEN: PLACE IN THE PRE-HEATED OVEN AT **220°C (425°F)**, AND BAKE FOR 10–15 MINUTES 220°C (425°F).
    WOOD FIRE OVEN: FOR BEST RESULTS, COOK AT THE MOUTH OF THE OVEN WHERE THERE IS THE LEAST HEAT. COOK AT 400°C (752°F) FOR 4–4.5 MINUTES.

8. Bake until the dough becomes puffed up, golden on top and the filling is hot. Serve immediately.

CALZONE CON FUNGHI AND OLIVES

Ingredients

- 40 g (1½ oz) dried porcini mushrooms
- Olive oil
- 1 garlic clove, minced
- 1 pepperoncino, chopped
- 40 g (1½ oz) field mushrooms, sliced
- 6 Ligurian olives, pitted
- Fresh oregano, chopped
- Fresh thyme, chopped
- 220 g (8 oz) pizza dough (see page 15)
- 60 g (2½ oz) Fior di Latte, cut into strips
- Salt and pepper

Method

1. If using a domestic oven, pre-heat to 220°C (425°F).
2. Soak the porcini in cold water for 2–3 minutes, then drain, keeping liquid aside.
3. In a large pan, heat some olive oil, adding the garlic and pepperoncino. Add the porcini mushrooms and reserved liquid, field mushrooms, fresh oregano and fresh thyme. Reduce until no liquid remains. Season with salt and pepper.
4. Roll out a piece of dough into a 3 mm thick disc, ensure the bottom of the dough is floured enough preventing it from sticking to the surface. On half of the dough piece place the Fior di Latte, the mushroom mix and olives, leaving a 5 cm (2 in) gap around the edge.
5. To make the calzone, carefully lift the far edge of the pizza dough and pull it over the top of the ingredients towards you, folding it in half. Crimp the edges so none of the filling can spill out.
6. Place the calzone onto a baking tray, pizza stone or granite slab.

   DOMESTIC OVEN: PLACE IN THE PRE-HEATED OVEN AT 220°C (425°F), AND BAKE FOR 10–15 MINUTES 220°C (425°F).
   WOOD FIRE OVEN: FOR BEST RESULTS, COOK AT THE MOUTH OF THE OVEN WHERE THERE IS THE LEAST HEAT. COOK AT 400°C (752°F) FOR 4–4.5 MINUTES.

7. Bake until the dough becomes puffed up, golden on top and the filling is hot. Serve immediately.

CALZONE CON PATATE, E CIPOLLA

Ingredients

- 100 g (3½ oz) potatoes, skin on and sliced thinly
- Drizzle of extra virgin olive oil
- Fresh rosemary, chopped
- 100 ml (3½ fl oz) olive oil
- 1 onion, chopped
- 1 teaspoon caster sugar (superfine sugar)
- 220 g (8 oz) pizza dough (see page 15)
- 60 g (2½ oz) Fior Di Latte, cut into strips
- Salt and pepper

Method

1. If using a domestic oven, pre-heat to 220°C (425°F).
2. Wash the potatoes in plenty of cold water to remove any field dust and soil. Slice the potatoes and place in a baking tray, drizzle with olive oil and season with the rosemary and salt and pepper to taste.
3. Oven bake at 130°C (266°F) for approximately for 15 minutes or until soft.
4. Heat the olive oil in a pan, add the chopped onion and sprinkle with a teaspoon of caster sugar. Cook on a low heat until the onions become caramelized.
5. Roll out a piece of dough into a 3 mm thick disc, ensure the bottom of the dough is floured enough preventing it from sticking to the surface. On half of the dough base place the Fior di latte across leaving a 5 cm (2 in) gap around the edge. Place the cooked potatoes and caramelized onion over the Fior di Latte.
6. To make the calzone, carefully lift the far edge of the pizza dough and pull it over the top of the ingredients towards you, folding it in half. Crimp the edges so none of the filling can spill out.
7. Place the calzone onto a baking tray, pizza stone or granite slab.

   DOMESTIC OVEN: PLACE IN THE PRE-HEATED OVEN AT 220°C (425°F), AND BAKE FOR 10–15 MINUTES 220°C (425°F).
   WOOD FIRE OVEN: FOR BEST RESULTS, COOK AT THE MOUTH OF THE OVEN WHERE THERE IS THE LEAST HEAT. COOK AT 400°C (752°F) FOR 4–4.5 MINUTES.

8. Bake until the dough becomes puffed up, golden on top and the filling is hot. Serve immediately.

CALZONE FRITTO CON BEEF NDUJA

Ingredients

- 220 g (8 oz) pizza dough (see page 15)
- 80 g (3 oz) Fior di Latte, cut into strips
- 60 g (2½ oz) Ricotta
- 50 g (2 oz) Beef Nduja, chopped
- 100 ml (3½ fl oz) olive oil
- Salt and pepper

Method

1. Roll out a piece of dough into a 3 mm thick disc, ensure the bottom of the dough is floured enough preventing it from sticking to the surface.
2. On one half of the pizza place the Fior di latte, Ricotta and Beef Nduja across leaving a 5 cm (2 in) gap around the edge. Season with salt and pepper.
3. To make the calzone, carefully lift the far edge of the pizza dough and pull it over the top of the ingredients towards you, folding it in half. Crimp the edges so none of the filling can spill out.
4. In a deep fryer, heat the oil to 300°C (572°F), place the calzone in the oil and fry until it becomes golden brown. Remove from the fryer and serve immediately.

CALZONE FRITTO CON TURKEY HAM E FUNGHI

Ingredients
- 220 g (8 oz) pizza dough (see page 15)
- 70 g (2½ oz) Fior di Latte
- 90 g (3 oz) Turkey ham
- 50 g (2 oz) mushrooms sliced
- 100 ml (3½ fl oz) olive oil
- Salt and pepper

Method
1. Roll out a piece of dough into a 3 mm thick disc, ensure the bottom of the dough is floured enough preventing it from sticking to the surface.
2. On one half of the pizza, place the Fior di latte, turkey ham and mushrooms across leaving a 5 cm (2 in) gap around the edge. Season with salt and pepper.
3. To make the calzone, carefully lift the far edge of the pizza dough and pull it over the top of the ingredients towards you, folding it in half. Crimp the edges so none of the filling can spill out.
4. Place the calzone in the deep fryer at 300°C (572°F) and fry until it becomes golden brown. Remove from the fryer and serve immediately.

DESSERT CALZONE
AND PIZZA

Two of my favourite things in the world come together here – pizza, and dessert.
Fruit or chocolate give a sweet spin on my classic recipes, and these desserts
can be as kid friendly, or as adults-only as you would like. What's not to love?

CALZONE ALLA NUTELLA

Ingredients
- 220 g (8 oz) pizza dough (see page 15)
- Nutella
- Sprinkle of icing sugar

Method
1. If using a domestic oven, pre-heat to 220°C (425°F).
2. Roll out a piece of dough into a 3 mm thick disc, ensure the bottom of the dough is floured enough preventing it from sticking to the surface. On half of the dough piece spread the Nutella (as much as you desire).
3. To make the calzone, carefully lift the far edge of the pizza dough and pull it over the top of the ingredients towards you, folding it in half. Crimp the edges so none of the filling can spill out.
4. Place the calzone onto a baking tray, pizza stone or granite slab.

   DOMESTIC OVEN: PLACE IN THE PRE-HEATED OVEN AT 220°C (425°F), AND BAKE FOR 10–15 MINUTES
   WOOD FIRE OVEN: FOR BEST RESULTS, COOK AT THE MOUTH OF THE OVEN WHERE THERE IS THE LEAST HEAT. COOK AT 400°C (752°F) FOR 4–4.5 MINUTES

5. Bake until the dough becomes puffed up, golden on top and the filling is hot. Serve hot, sprinkled with icing sugar and garnish with strawberries or fruit of your choice.

CALZONE CON FICHI E MASCARPONE

Ingredients

- 20 dried figs
- 300 ml (10 fl oz) red wine (non-alcoholic)
- 150 g (5 oz) white sugar
- 220 g (8 oz) pizza dough (see page 15)
- 1 tablespoon Mascarpone

Method

1. If using a domestic oven, pre-heat to 220°C (425°F).
2. Cut the dried figs into small pieces. Heat a saucepan over a low heat and add the non-alcoholic red wine and the sugar, then add the cut figs. Allow to reduce slowly until it reduces to at least half the amount. Allow to cool and strain the liquid (syrup) into a squeeze bottle. Keep the fig mix aside.
3. Roll out a piece of dough into a 3 mm thick disc, ensure the bottom of the dough is floured enough preventing it from sticking to the surface. On half of the dough piece spread the Mascarpone and evenly place the fig mix across the Mascarpone (as much as you desire).
4. To make the calzone, carefully lift the far edge of the pizza dough and pull it over the top of the ingredients towards you, folding it in half. Crimp the edges so none of the filling can spill out.
5. Place the calzone onto a baking tray, pizza stone or granite slab.

   DOMESTIC OVEN: PLACE IN THE PRE-HEATED OVEN AT 220°C (425°F), AND BAKE FOR 10–15 MINUTES
   WOOD FIRE OVEN: FOR BEST RESULTS, COOK AT THE MOUTH OF THE OVEN WHERE THERE IS THE LEAST HEAT. COOK AT 400°C (752°F) FOR 4–4.5 MINUTES

6. Bake until the dough becomes puffed up, golden on top and the filling is hot. Once cooked squeeze the syrup over the cooked calzone. Serve immediately.

CALZONE CON MELE, UVETTA E PINOLI

Ingredients

- 2 tablespoons unsalted butter
- 2 Golden Delicious apples, peeled, cored and diced
- 1 tablespoon raisins
- 2 tablespoons pine nuts
- 60 ml (2 fl oz) almond extract or Italian soda syrup
- 2 tablespoons brown sugar
- 1 tablespoon white or brown sugar
- 220 g (8 oz) pizza dough (see page 15)

Method

1. If using a domestic oven, pre-heat to 220°C (425°F).
2. Melt the butter in a small saucepan, add the apples, raisins and pine nuts.
3. Add the almond extract or Italian soda syrup, stir well and cook for approximately 10–15 minutes. Cook until the apples are soft and golden brown, then add the sugar and stir for 3–5 minutes or until the sugar has melted. Remove from the heat and allow to cool.
4. Roll out a piece of dough into a 3 mm thick disc, ensure the bottom of the dough is floured enough preventing it from sticking to the surface. Spread the apple mixture over half of the dough base.
5. To make the calzone, carefully lift the far edge of the pizza dough and pull it over the top of the ingredients towards you, folding it in half. Crimp the edges so none of the filling can spill out.
6. Place the calsone onto a baking tray, pizza stone or granite slab.

   DOMESTIC OVEN: PLACE IN THE PRE-HEATED OVEN AT 220°C (425°F), AND BAKE FOR 10–15 MINUTES
   WOOD FIRE OVEN: FOR BEST RESULTS, COOK AT THE MOUTH OF THE OVEN WHERE THERE IS THE LEAST HEAT. COOK AT 400°C (752°F) FOR 4–4.5 MINUTES

7. Bake until the dough becomes puffed up, golden on top and the filling is hot. Serve immediately.

RICOTTA, MIELE E MELE

Ingredients

- 2 Golden Delicious apples peeled and cored
- 20 g (½ oz) brown sugar
- 1 teaspoon cinnamon
- 2 tablespoons apricot or peach juice
- 220 g (8 oz) pizza dough (see page 15)

- 3 tablespoons honey
- 120 g (4½ oz) fresh Ricotta
- 30 g (1 oz) soft butter
- 3 springs of fresh thyme, chopped
- Walnuts, chopped

Method

1. If using a domestic oven, pre-heat to 220°C (425°F).
2. Peel and core the apples, cut in half and slice into 2 cm (¾ in) thick segments. Fan the apple separating the segments, then place in a bowl with the brown sugar, cinnamon and apricot or peach juice mix well and set aside for 5 minutes to soften.
3. Stretch the pizza dough into a round disk. Drizzle half of the honey over the base, then crumble the Ricotta evenly over the top.
4. Scoop out the apples from marinade and arrange on the pizza base. Drizzle over the remaining honey and place little knobs of butter evenly on top.
5. Add the fresh thyme then bake.

   DOMESTIC OVEN: PLACE IN THE PRE-HEATED OVEN AT 220°C (425°F), AND BAKE FOR 10–15 MINUTES
   WOOD FIRE OVEN: FOR BEST RESULTS, COOK AT THE MOUTH OF THE OVEN WHERE THERE IS THE LEAST HEAT FOR 90 SECONDS AT 400°C (752°F)

6. Once baked, serve hot and garnish with a sprinkling of chopped walnuts and any remaining honey.

PERE COTTE, CIOCCOLATO E MANDORLE

Ingredients

- 2 pears, peeled and cored
- 100 g (3½ oz) caster sugar (superfine sugar)
- 1.5 lt (5 fl oz) water
- 1 teaspoon mixed spice
- 3 tablespoons almond extract or Italian soda syrup
- 125 ml (4 fl oz) fine almond meal
- 30 g (1 oz) brown sugar

- 30 g (1 oz) butter
- 60 ml (2½ fl oz) thickened cream
- 40 g (1½ oz) dark chocolate
- 100 g (3½ oz) dark coverture chocolate buttons, plus extra for topping
- 220 g (8 oz) pizza dough (see page 15)
- 20 g (½ oz) almonds, slivered

Method

1. If using a domestic oven, pre-heat to 220°C (425°F).
2. In a medium saucepan, place the peeled pears, caster sugar, water, mixed spice and almond extract or Italian soda syrup. Over medium heat, bring to the boil, then immediately turn it down to a very soft simmer for around 10 minutes or until your pears come off the knife when you try and lift them. Turn off the heat and set aside.
3. In a bowl mix together the almond meal, brown sugar and butter to form a paste.
4. Place the cream in a small saucepan over a medium heat. When it begins to boil turn off the flame and add the dark chocolate buttons. Let it stand for 3 minutes then slowly mix till smooth and shiny.
5. Stretch the pizza dough into a round disk. Spread your almond meal mixture evenly over the base in a thin layer.
6. Drain and slice the poached pears, arrange on the pizza base evenly and in the spare spaces place the extra chocolate buttons.
7. Drizzle 2 tablespoons of the poaching juice on top of the pizza, add the almonds then bake.

    DOMESTIC OVEN: PLACE IN THE PRE-HEATED OVEN AT 220°C (425°F), AND BAKE FOR 10–15 MINUTES
    WOOD FIRE OVEN: FOR BEST RESULTS, COOK AT THE MOUTH OF THE OVEN WHERE THERE IS THE LEAST HEAT FOR 90 SECONDS AT 400°C (752°F)

8. Once cooked, garnish the pizza with the chocolate and cream mix.

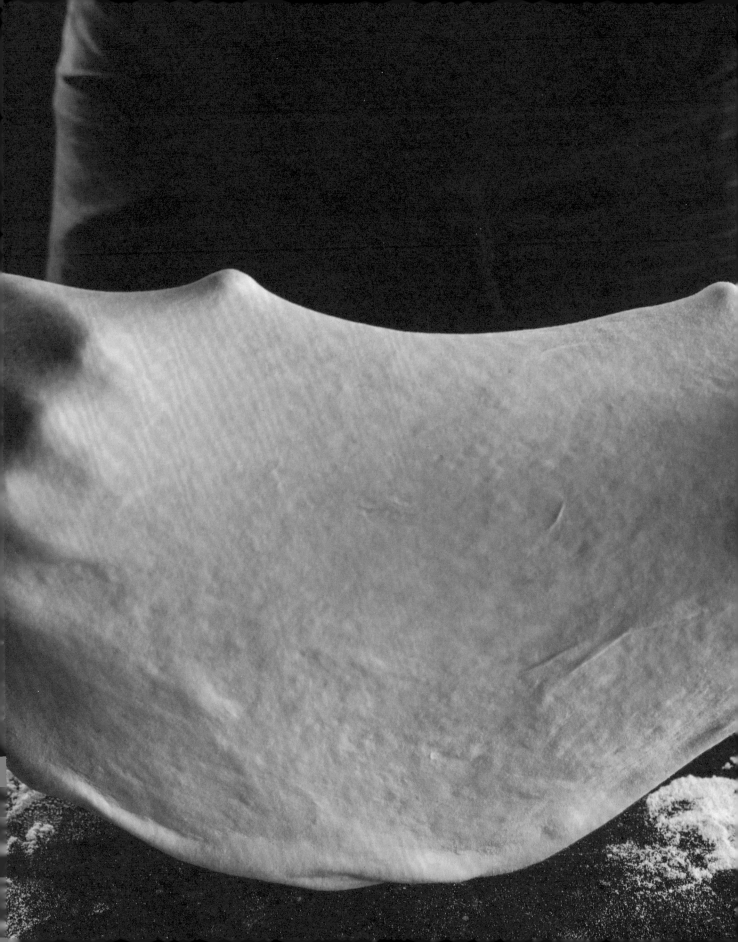

Index

This book is dedicated to my family; to my beautiful, patient, understanding wife Maria, and our three gorgeous children. Without your love and support, none of this would be possible.

First published in 2015 by New Holland Publishers
Sydney

Level 1, 178 Fox Valley Road, Wahroonga, NSW 2076, Australia

newhollandpublishers.com

A record of this book is held at the National Library of Australia.

ISBN 9781742577227

Managing Director: Fiona Schultz
Publisher: Diane Ward
Project Editor: Holly Willsher
Designer: Andrew Quinlan
Production Director: Arlene Gippert
Photography: Greg Elms
Food Stylist: Kirsty Bryson
Printed in China

10 9 8 7 6 5

Keep up with New Holland Publishers:
 NewHollandPublishers
 @newhollandpublishers